THE STORY BEHIND

OIL

Heidi Moore

Raintree

www.raintreepublishers.co.uk
Visit our website to find out more information about Raintree books.

To order:
☎ Phone 0845 6044371
🖷 Fax +44 (0) 1865 312263
✉ Email myorders@capstonepub.co.uk

Customers from outside the UK please telephone +44 1865 312262

Raintree is an imprint of Capstone Global Library Limited, a company incorporated in England and Wales having its registered office at 7 Pilgrim Street, London, EC4V 6LB – Registered company number: 6695582

"Raintree" is a registered trademark of Pearson Education Limited, under licence to Capstone Global Library Limited.

Text © Capstone Global Library Limited 2009
First published in hardback in 2009
Paperback edition first published in 2010
The moral rights of the proprietor have been asserted.

Edited by Louise Galpine, David Andrews, and Laura Knowles
Designed by Philippa Jenkins and Artistix
Original illustrations © Capstone Global Library Ltd
Illustrated by Phil Gleaves/Specs Art
Picture research by Mica Brancic and Elaine Willis
Originated by Modern Age Repro House Ltd.
Printed in China by CTPS

ISBN 978 0 431114 87 3 (hardback)
13 12 11 10 09
10 9 8 7 6 5 4 3 2 1

ISBN 978 0 431115 02 3 (paperback)
14 13 12 11 10
10 9 8 7 6 5 4 3 2 1

British Library Cataloguing in Publication Data
Moore, Heidi
The story behind oil. – (True stories)
665.5
A full catalogue record for this book is available from the British Library.

Acknowledgements
We would like to thank the following for permission to reproduce photographs: © akg-images p. 13; Alamy p. 10 (© LE Robshaw); Art Archive p. 16 (© Culver Pictures); Corbis pp. 6 (© Patrice Latron), 8 (© Stephanie Maze), 21 (© Hulton-Deutsch Collection), 27 (© Owaki – Kulla); Getty Images pp. 4 (© Dr. Marli Miller), 19 (Hulton Archive/© Fox Photos), 23 (© AFP/HLA HLA HTAY), 24 (Stone/© Ulf Wallin), 25 (Stone/© Ben Osborne); iStock p. iii (© Mark Evans 2008); © Mary Evans Picture Library pp. 15, 18; Photolibrary p. 26 (age fotostock/© Christophe Canato); Photolibrary.com p. 7 (© Lucidio Inc); Science Photo Library pp. 5 (© Cordelia Molloy), 20 (© US Air Force); © The Bridgeman Art Library p. 12 (Prado, Madrid, Spain).

Cover photograph of an oil worker collecting oil in a Northern suburb of Baku, Azerbaijan (1998) reproduced with permission of Corbis (© Remi Benali).

Every effort has been made to contact copyright holders of any material reproduced in this book. Any omissions will be rectified in subsequent printings if notice is given to the publisher.

All the Internet addresses (URLs) given in this book were valid at the time of going to press. However, due to the dynamic nature of the Internet, some addresses may have changed, or sites may have changed or ceased to exist since publication. While the author and Publishers regret any inconvenience this may cause readers, no responsibility for any such changes can be accepted by either the author or the publishers.

Contents

Some words are shown in bold, **like this**.
You can find out what they mean by
looking in the glossary.

Oil from Earth

▲ Oil bubbles up from sources in the ground.

Imagine Earth about 600 million years ago. The only living creatures were tiny animals in the oceans and seas. This was before dinosaurs roamed the planet, and millions of years before human life. When these tiny living things died, they fell to the ocean floor. They were buried along with plants and other **organic matter** (natural substances).

Over many millions of years, layers and layers of silt formed on top of the remains. Silt is soil at the bottom of the sea or ocean. High heat and pressure from deep within Earth went to work on the organic matter. These forces changed the matter into oil.

A day without oil

Today, oil is one of the most important substances on Earth. Try to imagine a day without it. There would be no cars, trains, or buses. All of those things run on oil. You would have to walk or ride your bike everywhere. But your bike would probably have different tyres. Most tyres are made partly from oil.

You could not chew gum. Chewing gum is made partly from oil. You could not use crayons to draw pictures. Even crayons contain a product made from oil!

Look around your home and try to count all the things that are made from oil. It is used for much more than just fuel for cars.

▼ **All these products are made from oil.**

Energy trapped underground

▲ Oil comes in different shades, from clear to very dark.

Many different products are called oils. There are the oils we eat, such as peanut oil and olive oil. It is fairly easy to get these kinds of oil. Peanut oil comes from pressing peanuts, and olive oil comes from pressing olives. But the oil used to power cars takes much, much longer to form.

Over millions of years, extreme heat and pressure deep inside Earth change **organic matter** into oil. You might think of oil as being black, but it can be clear, light brown, or dark brown as well.

Petroleum

Another term for oil is **petroleum**. The word *petroleum* actually refers to three separate substances:

- **natural gas**: a gas that is used in homes to cook food and heat water

- **crude oil**: the liquid form of petroleum before it is turned into petrol and other products

- **bitumen**: a thick and tar-like solid form of oil.

▼ Natural gas is another form of fuel. It can be used to cook food on a hob.

▼ These men are working at an oil well. They drill deep into the ground to find oil.

Fossil fuels

Crude oil and natural gas are **fossil fuels**. They are important sources of **energy**, or usable power. The term *fossil fuel* comes from the process that turns dead plant and animal matter into oil. (The remains of dead plants and animals are called fossils.) Another name for fossil fuel is mineral fuel.

So, there are three types of petroleum: natural gas, crude oil, and bitumen. But what is petroleum? Petroleum is mostly made up of hydrocarbons, which are **compounds** of hydrogen and carbon. On its own, hydrogen is a gas. Carbon by itself is a hard solid. When the two combine, it creates petroleum. Petroleum also contains some nitrogen, sulphur, and oxygen.

Trees and plants contain hydrocarbons as well. Hydrocarbons are **flammable** (able to be burned). This is what makes them good for fuel. Car engines and other machines burn fuel to produce energy.

The oil window

Petroleum occurs deep within Earth at depths of about 760 to 4,880 metres (2,500 to 16,000 feet). The best place to find crude oil is at depths of 2,000 to 2,900 metres (6,600 to 9,500 feet). This is called the oil window.

Because petroleum is lighter than water, it moves up through groundwater and fills cracks and holes in rocks. These cracks and holes are gas traps. Drilling down into a gas trap releases the oil for use.

▼ **This diagram shows how oil formed in Earth's crust.**

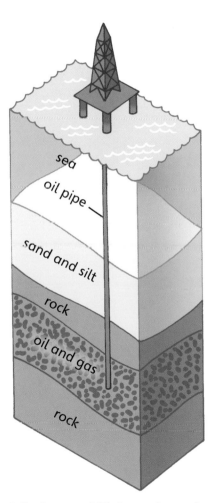

1 Millions of years ago, plants and sea creatures died and were buried by layers of sand and silt on the ocean floor.

2 Over millions of years the remains were buried deeper and deeper. Heat and pressure turned them into oil and gas.

3 Today we drill down through layers of sand, silt, and rock to reach the layer of rock containing oil and gas.

Discovery and early use

▶ This model mammoth was put in the La Brea tar pits to show how animals became stuck long ago.

People have known about **crude oil** for perhaps as long as 5,000 years. The earliest known sources of **petroleum** were surface pools known as **oil seeps**. At these sources, pools of oil bubble up from deep inside the ground.

It's the pits!

The La Brea tar pits in Los Angeles, California, USA, are a famous oil seep. You can still visit them today. Scientists have found the remains of plants and animals from millions of years ago in the tar pits. The animals, such as mammoths, got trapped in the tar.

3000–1000 BCE
The ancient Egyptians use crude oil for many purposes, such as a way to preserve the dead as mummies.

2000 BCE
The ancient Mesopotamians collect crude oil and asphalt from oil seeps.

3000 BCE

2000 BCE

Ancient Mesopotamians, living in what is now the Middle East, collected crude oil and **asphalt**. Asphalt is also known as tar and is a thick black material. It is often used for building. Today, asphalt is used for lining roads and making roof shingles.

The ancient Egyptians used crude oil for many different things. They used it to dress (bandage) wounds and to get rid of aches and pains in the body.

In the ancient world, people also used oil to make weapons of war. Persians, living in what is now Iran, shot arrows wrapped in oil-soaked rags. They would set the rags alight and then launch the fiery arrows at their enemies.

▼ The brown areas on this map show some of the places where oil has been found.

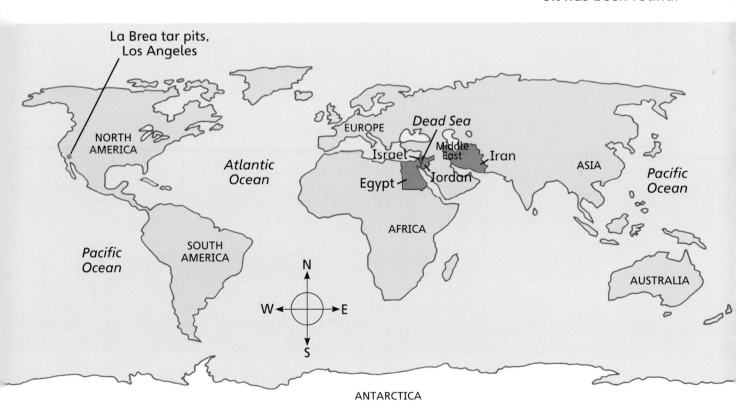

480 BCE
Persians (in what is now Iran) use oil to make weapons of war, lighting oil-soaked rags to shoot on arrows.

1000 BCE

The oil age

▲ This painting shows ancient war ships using Greek fire.

By the 1300s, people were using **crude oil** to make new materials. They would **distill** the **petroleum** by heating it until it boiled. Then they cooled the vapour (gas) it gave off. People used this product to make medicine and other things.

Greek fire

Another product made by distilling petroleum is naphtha. It is a liquid similar to petrol. The ancient Greeks used the term *naphtha* to mean ordinary crude oil. They would throw this **flammable** material at their enemies. The substance became known as "Greek fire".

1300s
New uses of crude oil develop along with the distillation process.

Eager for fuel

The real oil age began hundreds of years later, from around 1760 to 1850. During that time, the **Industrial Revolution** brought about big changes in Great Britain, the United States, , and other western countries. New technology changed the way people lived and worked. Work that was once done by hand was now done by machines. Steam engines powered huge ships across vast oceans.

All these changes made people eager for a new source of fuel. This was before electricity. People would rely on oil lamps at night. The lamps often burned whale oil, but this was expensive and hard to get. Candles made from tallow (animal fat) gave off a bad smell.

In about 1850 a Canadian doctor named Abraham Gesner worked out a way to produce a new fuel. He made it by distilling crude oil. This new product, **kcroscnc**, was a cheap and useful fuel for lamps.

▼ Many factories developed during the Industrial Revolution.

1760–1850	1850	
The Industrial Revolution changes people's needs for fuel.	Canadian doctor Abraham Gesner makes the cheap lamp fuel kerosene out of crude oil.	13

1600   1700   1800   1900

The first oil well

In 1859 a US oil driller called Edwin L. Drake drilled the first oil well in the United States. It was in Titusville, Pennsylvania. This event started the US petroleum boom.

How an oil well works

To make an oil well, first an oil rig was set up. This had a large support structure called a derrick and a drill. The derrick would send a long drill bit deep into the ground. If the drill bit struck oil, a huge jet of oil would shoot into the air.

Then pumping would begin. An oil pump with a sucker rod would be placed on the well head. The motor would bring up the oil from the ground. The front of an oil pump is called the horse head. It is shaped a bit like a horse's head and neck.

▼ Here you can see how an oil pump works. A motor moves the walking beam, which moves the sucker rod up and down. This pumps oil out of the well and through the pipe.

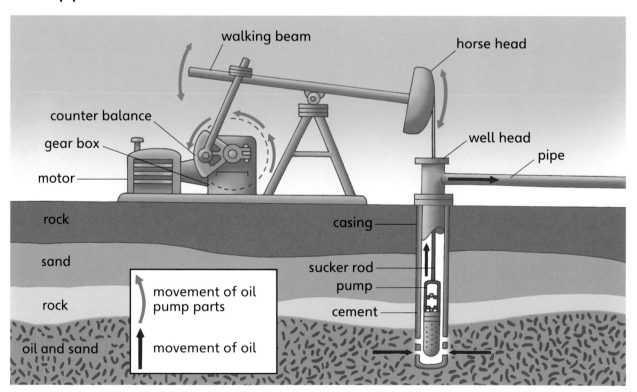

walking beam • horse head • counter balance • gear box • well head • pipe • motor • rock • casing • sand • sucker rod • pump • rock • cement • oil and sand

movement of oil pump parts

movement of oil

1859
US oil driller Edwin L. Drake drills the first oil well in the United States in Titusville, Pennsylvania.

1870s
Kerosene is used throughout the world.

Demand for crude oil

By the 1870s, people all over the world were using kerosene to light streetlamps and lamps in the home. This meant that the demand for crude oil increased. But there was still no good way to use one of the main products made from the distilling process – petrol. It was too flammable to use to heat the home. It would have been too dangerous.

By the end of the 1800s, oil fields had been discovered in Europe, the United States, and East Asia.

Oil today

Every day about 80 million barrels of oil are transported from oil fields around the world.

◀ **In this drawing from the 1800s, a man lights a kerosene streetlamp.**

late 1800s

Oil fields are discovered in Europe, the United States, and East Asia.

Meet a famous oilman

In 1863 John D. Rockefeller started an oil refinery to process crude oil. He went on to found the Standard Oil Company, a very large and important oil company. In the 1890s about 80 per cent of the petroleum business in the United States was controlled by Standard Oil.

▶ This photograph of John D. Rockefeller was taken in around 1907.

Black gold

By the 1880s, oil was a very important product. Because of its high value, people called it black gold. Another name for it was Texas tea, because it was found in large amounts in Texas, USA.

The oil boom made a few people very wealthy. Before long, people from far and wide were travelling to the United States to try their luck at discovering oil. These people were called oil prospectors.

Finding oil was not easy. Some people drilled for years and did not find anything. Many spent all their money in the process.

1863

US businessman John D. Rockefeller, the founder of Standard Oil, starts an oil refinery to process crude oil.

Refining oil

Many prospectors became wealthy by creating oil **refineries** (see diagram). Oil **refining** separates crude oil into different substances. The oldest and most common refining method is distilling. Newer processes use chemicals to break down oil into different substances. These substances become different petroleum products, such as petrol.

▼ This diagram shows how an oil refinery works. Crude oil is heated until it turns into a vapour. As it cools down, it is distilled into different oil products.

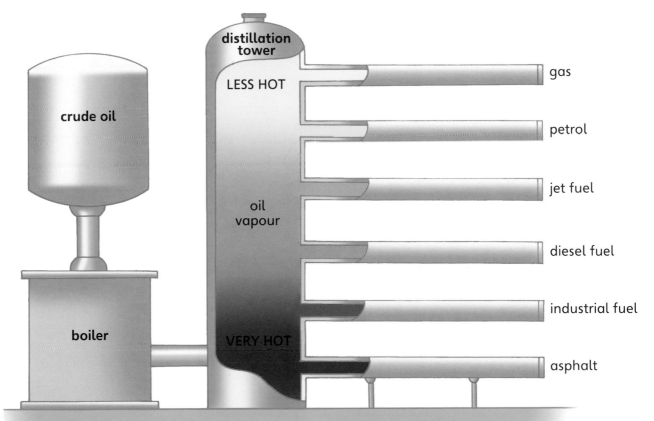

crude oil

distillation tower

LESS HOT

oil vapour

boiler

VERY HOT

gas

petrol

jet fuel

diesel fuel

industrial fuel

asphalt

late 1800s
The oil boom makes many people wealthy.

Age of the automobile

▲ This 1882 drawing shows an oil refinery in Russia.

In 1876 a German inventor called Nikolaus Otto came up with a new type of engine. It was an internal combustion engine. *Internal* means "inside", and *combustion* means "burning".

The internal combustion engine ran on petrol. Before that, most engines were powered by steam. But steam engines had to be very large to do much work. Even a small internal combustion engine could do a lot of work.

Diesel or petrol?

Diesel engines are more **efficient** than petrol engines. They do more work with less fuel. Diesel fuel is also not as **flammable**. These types of engines are still popular in Europe.

But most US cars run on petrol, not diesel fuel. This is because diesel fuel used to contain large amounts of sulphur. Sulphur is a smelly chemical that **pollutes** the air. US carmakers switched to petrol. But many other countries, such as Great Britain, later changed to a form of diesel with very low sulphur. Some US carmakers are bringing back diesel-fuelled cars.

1876
German inventor Nikolaus Otto creates the internal combustion engine.

1885
German engineer Karl Benz builds the first motor carriage powered by a gas engine.

1850   1900

First motor carriage

A few years later, in 1885, a German engineer called Karl Benz built a carriage powered by a petrol engine. This was the world's first car! His invention changed transport forever.

In 1908 US businessman Henry Ford built the Model T car. Mass production of cars began after that. People in factories were able to make lots of cars quickly and cheaply. Owning a car was soon within reach for many people.

▼ These motorists are refuelling their car at an early petrol station in Blashford, England.

1908
US businessman Henry Ford builds the Model T, the first widely affordable car.

Planes, trains, and automobiles

After the car was invented, the demand for petrol increased. Not that long before, petrol was a useless product made from oil **refining**. Now it was fast becoming one of the most important goods in the world.

Oil also changed the way goods were shipped. Before the diesel engine was invented, trains ran on coal. Then trains switched to diesel engines. Diesel fuel was cheaper, cleaner, and more powerful than coal. Ships that were once powered by coal now ran on diesel as well.

Today, high petrol prices have made electric cars and hybrid cars a smart choice. Hybrid cars run on both petrol and electric power.

▶ Orville Wright piloting a later version of his aeroplane in 1913.

1900	1903	1920
One-third of cars in the United States are electric.	Orville and Wilbur Wright make the world's first successful aeroplane flight in Kitty Hawk, North Carolina, USA.	The electric car goes out of production in the United States due to lack of demand.

1900

The electric car

Electric cars have been around since the 1830s. By 1900 about 30 per cent of the cars in the United States were electric. But in 1908 the cheap, petrol-powered Model T came out. At the same time, petrol stations were popping up all over Europe and the United States. Easy access to petrol made petrol cars more popular. Electric cars have to be charged at a power source. They cannot travel very far on a single charge.

▲ Around 1900 US inventor Thomas Edison tried to design a more powerful battery to power electric cars.

1950s
People regularly use aeroplanes to travel around the world.

2000s
Electric cars and hybrid cars become popular.

1950

2000

The problem with petroleum

Today, it takes a huge amount of **petroleum** to power the world. In 2007 people used about 86 million barrels of **crude oil** a day. What if this supply runs out? Many scientists think that will happen in the future.

Maximum oil production is called peak oil. After that, oil supplies will begin to run out. Some think the world will reach that point soon. Rapid growth in countries such as China and India mean oil **reserves** are disappearing quickly. The United States also consumes oil at a very high rate. The United States has less than 5 per cent of the world's population, but it uses 25 per cent of the world's crude oil.

▶ **This diagram shows how much of a barrel of crude oil goes into different products.**

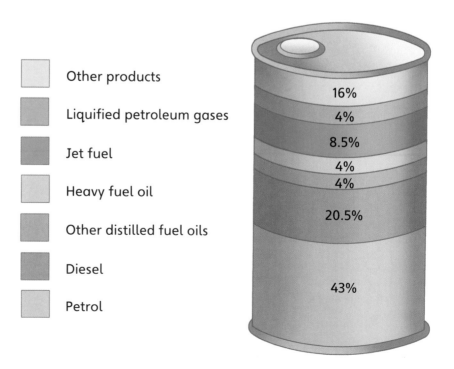

Other products

Liquified petroleum gases

Jet fuel

Heavy fuel oil

Other distilled fuel oils

Diesel

Petrol

16%

4%

8.5%

4%

4%

20.5%

43%

Worldwide oil crisis?

Some experts think that by 2015, oil supplies will not be able to keep up with demand. Because oil takes millions of years to form in the earth, we cannot simply create more. Oil is a non-renewable resource. When it runs out, it runs out forever. Many believe there will be a worldwide oil crisis.

▲ Long lines of cars built up when drivers tried to buy petrol during a petrol shortage in Myanmar in 2008.

Petrol shortages ✔

Many countries have already faced petrol shortages. The 1973 oil crisis in the United Kingdom led to record-high petrol prices. Drivers queued up outside petrol stations to fill their tanks. Many petrol stations ran out of petrol.

Pollution

Another problem with petroleum is that it **pollutes** the air. Anything that burns **fossil fuels** releases the gas carbon dioxide into the air.

Carbon dioxide is not harmful on its own. It occurs in nature, and plants need it to live. But it is a problem when too much of the gas builds up. Carbon dioxide is a **greenhouse gas**. It absorbs heat from the sun. This process can lead to global warming, which is a rise in worldwide temperatures.

▶ Smog hangs over the city of Los Angeles, USA. Smog is formed in the atmosphere when fumes from cars and factories are acted on by sunlight.

Oil and unrest

A further problem with oil is connected with where it is found. Many countries with oil reserves are in unstable regions, such as the Middle East. Some oil-producing countries are led by dangerous rulers. This has led to wars and other unrest over oil.

The problem with global warming

Hotter weather does not sound so bad at first. But it would have a huge effect on Earth. Even an increase of just 2°C (3.6°F) worldwide could melt the polar ice caps (the large areas of ice at the North and South poles). If this were to happen, the ocean would rise to dangerous levels. Some areas of the world would flood, and others would become deserts. Many species (types) of animals would die out.

Big spill!

Oil spills can cause terrible harm. In 1989 the *Exxon Valdez* oil tanker ran aground along the coast of Alaska. It dumped 41 million litres (11 million gallons) of crude oil. That is enough oil to fill 124 Olympic-size swimming pools. The oil spread over 2,100 kilometres (1,300 miles) of coastline and killed hundreds of thousands of animals, including bald eagles, seals, and sea otters.

▼ A worker rescues a seabird harmed in an oil spill.

The future of oil

▲ Riding your bike instead of using a car helps reduce the amount of fossil fuels burned.

Today, the oil industry (business) is trying to solve the problem of supply. Some people want to increase the supply of **petroleum**. They are exploring new sources of oil.

One new source of oil is tar sands. These areas contain thick, heavy oil called **bitumen**. It is very difficult to get the petroleum from the tar sands. The process requires lots of **energy**. Using energy to get a product that **pollutes** is very wasteful. It creates two to four times the amount of **greenhouse gases** per barrel as ordinary oil!

Better sources of energy

Many people believe that new sources of oil are not the answer. A better way to solve the energy crisis is to switch to renewable resources. These are energy sources such as wind, water, and sunshine that never run out.

◀ These wind **turbines** turn wind power into energy.

Renewable resources could supply us with enough energy to power Earth. It would also create far less pollution. Today, the technology is still costly. But the more people demand renewable energy, the cheaper and more widespread it will become.

Where is the oil?	
Top five oil producers (in 2007):	
Saudi Arabia	11 million barrels per day
Russia	9.9 million barrels per day
United States	7.5 million barrels per day
Iran	4 million barrels per day
China	3.7 million barrels per day
Top five countries with biggest oil reserves:	
Saudi Arabia	264 billion barrels
Canada	179 billion barrels
Iran	136 billion barrels
Iraq	113 billion barrels
Kuwait	102 billion barrels

Pain at the pump ✔

Oil prices have risen sharply in the past 10 years. Oil is usually priced in US dollars. The price of oil climbed from $32 a barrel in 1991 to nearly $150 in 2008. This drove up petrol prices. Today, it is very expensive to own a large, petrol-guzzling car. Smaller, fuel-**efficient** cars are better for the environment and cheaper to run. Of course, it is even cheaper and better for the environment to walk, ride a bike, or take the bus or train.

Timeline

(These dates are often approximations.)

3000–1000 BCE
The ancient Egyptians use **crude oil** for many purposes, such as a way to preserve the dead as mummies.

3000 BCE   2500 BCE

1556
German scientist Georg Bauer (Georgius Agricola) first uses the word *petroleum*.

1300s
New uses of crude oil develop along with the process of **distilling**.

1500   1000

1760–1850
The Industrial Revolution changes people's needs for fuel.

1800

late 1800s
Oil fields are discovered in Europe, the United States, and East Asia. The oil boom makes many people wealthy.

1885
German inventor Karl Benz builds the first motor carriage powered by a petrol engine.

1876
German inventor Nikolaus Otto creates the internal combustion engine.

1900
One-third of cars in the United States are electric.

1903
Orville and Wilbur Wright make the world's first successful aeroplane flight in Kitty Hawk, North Carolina, USA.

1908
US businessman Henry Ford builds the Model T, the first widely affordable car.

1900

1991
Oil costs $32 a barrel.

1989
Oil tanker the *Exxon Valdez* runs aground in Alaska and dumps 41 million litres (11 million gallons) of crude oil.

early 2000s
Electric cars and hybrid cars become popular.

2007
The world consumes 86 million barrels of crude oil a day.

2008
Oil prices climb to nearly $150 per barrel.

2000

28   This symbol shows where there is a change of scale in the timeline, or where a long period of time with no noted events has been left out.

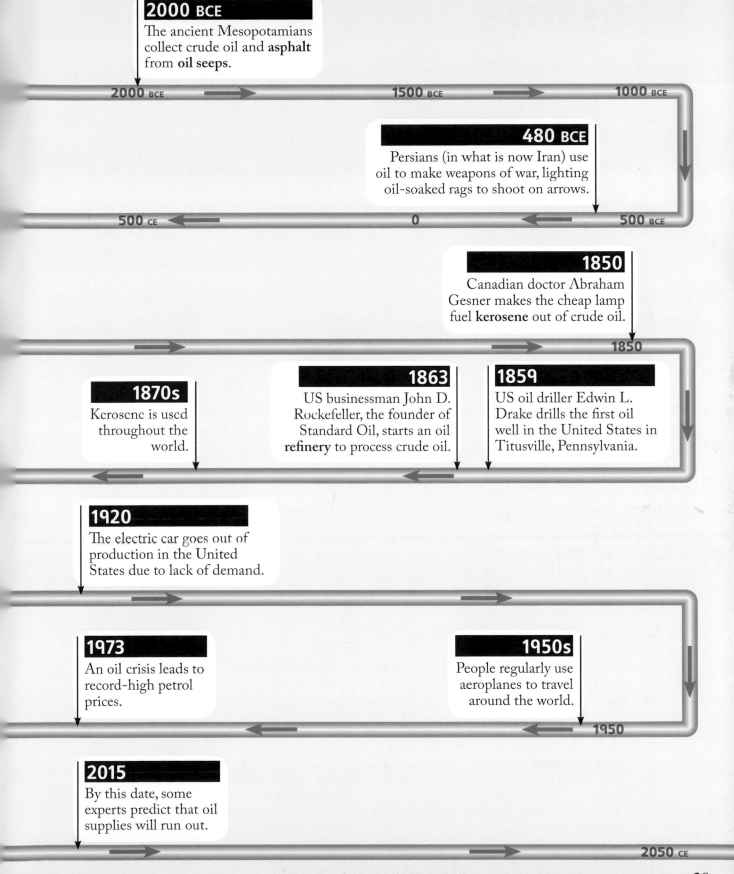

2000 BCE
The ancient Mesopotamians collect crude oil and **asphalt** from **oil seeps**.

2000 BCE   1500 BCE   1000 BCE

480 BCE
Persians (in what is now Iran) use oil to make weapons of war, lighting oil-soaked rags to shoot on arrows.

500 CE   0   500 BCE

1850
Canadian doctor Abraham Gesner makes the cheap lamp fuel **kerosene** out of crude oil.

1850

1870s
Kerosene is used throughout the world.

1863
US businessman John D. Rockefeller, the founder of Standard Oil, starts an oil **refinery** to process crude oil.

1859
US oil driller Edwin L. Drake drills the first oil well in the United States in Titusville, Pennsylvania.

1920
The electric car goes out of production in the United States due to lack of demand.

1973
An oil crisis leads to record-high petrol prices.

1950s
People regularly use aeroplanes to travel around the world.

1950

2015
By this date, some experts predict that oil supplies will run out.

2050 CE

Glossary

asphalt thick black form of petroleum; sometimes called tar or bitumen. Asphalt is often used to cover roads.

BCE meaning "before the common era". When this appears after a date, it refers to the time before the Christian religion began. BCE dates are always counted backwards.

bitumen thick black form of petroleum; sometimes called tar or asphalt. Bitumen has been used in building for thousands of years.

CE meaning "common era". When this appears after a date, it refers to the time after the Christian religion began.

compound substance made up of two or more chemicals bonded (combined) together

crude oil liquid form of petroleum. Crude oil prices have been rising sharply in recent years.

distill separate something into different substances by boiling it and then cooling the steam it gives off. Distilling crude oil produces petrol, jet fuel, and diesel.

efficient do more work with less energy. Diesel engines are more efficient than many petrol engines.

energy usable power, such as heat or electricity. Fuel supplies energy to run machines.

flammable able to be burned. Petrol is a very flammable fuel.

fossil fuel fuel made from the remains of dead plants and animals. Coal and oil are fossil fuels.

greenhouse gas gas that absorbs heat from the sun and warms the environment. Carbon dioxide is a greenhouse gas.

Industrial Revolution time period when people first began making and using fuel-powered machines to do work on a large scale

kerosene product made from petroleum. In the late 1800s kerosene was used to fuel lamps.

natural gas gas form of petroleum. Natural gas is used in homes to cook food and heat water.

oil seep place where crude oil bubbles up to the surface of the ground. Ancient peoples collected crude oil at oil seeps.

organic matter plant and animal material. Crude oil comes from heat and pressure acting on organic matter over millions of years.

petroleum rock oil. Petroleum comes from deep inside Earth.

pollute poison or make dirty. Burning oil pollutes the air.

refine free from unwanted material. People refine oil to get petrol.

refinery plant where something is processed. Crude oil is processed in a refinery.

reserve amount of material set aside for later use. As more and more people drive cars, oil reserves are getting smaller.

turbine machine that spins to turn motion into energy. Wind turbines spin to turn the motion of the wind into electrical energy.

Find out more

Books

Fuelling the Future: Fossil Fuels and Biofuels, Elizabeth Raum (Heinemann Library, 2008)

Oil, John Farndon (Dorling Kindersley, 2007)

Potato Clocks and Solar Cars: Renewable and Non-renewable Energy, Elizabeth Raum (Raintree, 2007)

Websites

Learn how oil formed and about the ways we use oil today on this site run by the US Department of Energy.
www.eia.doe.gov/kids/energyfacts/sources/non-renewable/oil.html

Read the World Almanac for Kids' chapter on petroleum. To get to it, click on the Chapter Article link for "petroleum" on this web page:
www.worldalmanacforkids.com/WAKI-Chapter.aspx?chapter_id=4

This website tells you all about fossil fuels and where they come from.
www.carbonkids.net/kids_fossilfuels.html

Index